THE
$1.00 WORD
RIDDLE BOOK

Riddles by

Marilyn Burns

Pictures by

Martha Weston

MATH SOLUTIONS PUBLICATIONS

Book Design by William S. Wells

Printed in the United States of America

ISBN 0-941355-02-0

Distributed by Cuisenaire Company of America, Inc.
P.O. Box 5026
White Plains, New York 10602-5026
(800) 237-3142
FAX (800) 551-7637

Introduction

This is no ordinary riddle book. Figuring out the answers to the riddles in this book calls for more than just thinking about words. It calls for doing some mathematics also. That's because the answers to all the riddles in this book are $1.00 words.

How can we tell?

WOW! That's expensive!

How you can tell if an answer is a $1.00 word?

It's simple.
Use a = $.01, b = $.02, c = $.03, and so on up to
z = $.26, and add the value of each letter in the word. If
the sum is $1.00, then the word is worth $1.00.

"Riddle," for example, is worth $.52. Not enough for
a $1.00 word.

"Zoology" is worth $1.15. Too much. You're looking for
words that are exactly $1.00.

Maybe your name is worth $1.00. That's how Henrietta
got to be on the cover of this book.
(Check for yourself to see that "Henrietta" really is
a $1.00 word.)

That's also how the elephants got there. As a matter of
fact, each of the words in the caption on the cover about
Henrietta and the elephants is a $1.00 word.

At this time, several hundred $1.00 words have been
found by addition-loving kids across the United States.
The riddles in this book give you clues to more
than 100 of them.

About the Riddles

Some of the riddles are drawings like the cover
illustration of Henrietta and the elephants. However, the
captions on these riddles are incomplete. Your job is to
figure out the $1.00 word that fits in each blank.
Here's an example.

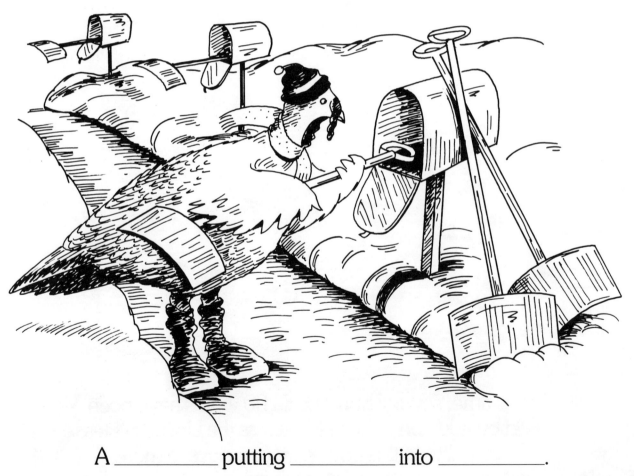

A _____ putting _____ into _____.

Some riddles are drawings without captions. For these, the answer is just one $1.00 word. Try this sample.

_____

In other riddles, you get your clues from words instead of from pictures. Try this one.

What's a blue-green color?

(It's not "turquoise." That's worth $1.45.)

———————————————

I wonder what's the most expensive color I could find.

Also, there's a story in the book about Robin Hood. You probably know about Robin Hood's escapades of stealing from the rich to give to the poor, but you probably haven't heard about the rock band he started. You'll learn about Robin Hood and the Hot-Blooded Hawkers, and have the chance to find the forty-two $1.00 words in the story. (If you're wondering why Robin Hood belongs in this book, it's because he has a $1.00 name. "Hot-blooded" and "Hawkers" are each $1.00 words as well.)

There's a special bonus at the end of the book. It's a computer program, written in BASIC, that will work on Apple and IBM computers. You may find it handy.

THE
RIDDLES...

A _____1_____ **on the beach** _____2_____ _____3_____ .

4 _____

5 _____

The _____7_____ are _____8_____ _____9_____ .

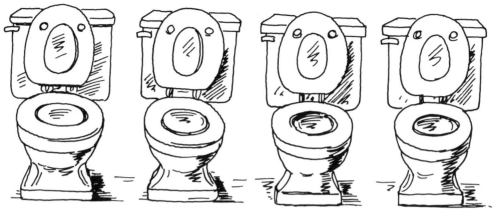

10

11

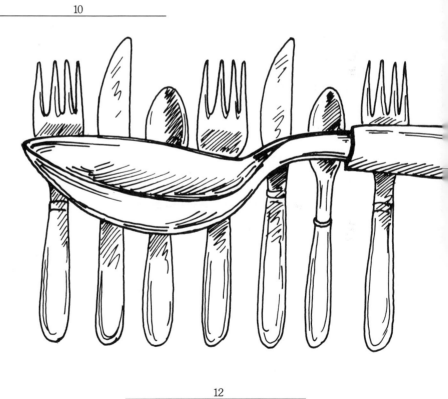

12

13 _____ **ing**

14 _____ **ing**

15 _____ **ing**

16 _____ **ing**

17

18

19

How can you describe a machine that works without people having to press buttons?

_____ 20 _____

What's a particular golf club?

_____ 21 _____

What's the verdict for a suspect who's found not guilty?

_____ 22 _____

Who discovered how to make milk safe to drink?

_____ 23 _____

What can you use so glasses don't leave rings on tables?

24

What miner's daughter had a song named after her?

25

What do you call the last few games to decide who wins the pennant?

26

What do you call verses in a song?

27

_____ 28 _____ 29 _____ **wearing**

_____ **riding on** _____ .
    30   31

_____32_____ **iest**

_____33_____ **iest**

_____ 35 _____ **iest**

_____ 34 _____ **iest**

_____ 36 _____ **iest**

A _____ 37 _____ 38 **on a** _____ 39 **wearing** _____ 40 .

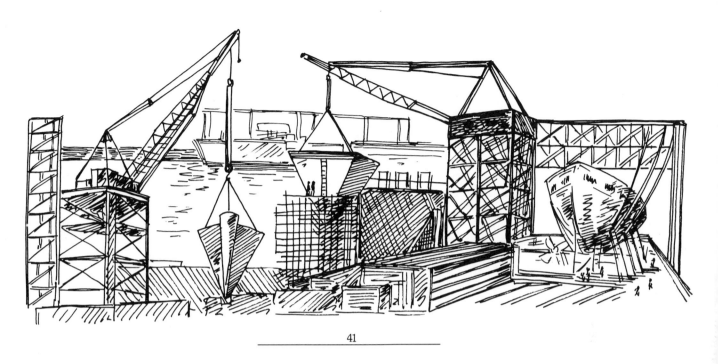

41

42

43

What do you call the United States Senate and House of Representatives together?

44

What did the tennis player do when she hit the ball before it bounced?

45

What's the opposite of minimize?

46

What describes how a snake gets to the other side of the road?

What's used to figure discounts?

48

How can you describe meat that hasn't been cooked long enough?

49

What do you need to do to the following sentence so the reader knows who's doing the asking?

Where are you going Henry asked Jenny

50

_____ 51 _____ **ing**

_____ 52 _____ **ing**

_____ 53 _____ **ing**

_____ 54 _____ **ing**

_____ 55 _____ **ing**

_____ 56 _____ **ing**

58

59

60

61

62

63

_____ 64 _____ **wearing** _____ 65 _____ **and** _____ 66 _____ **their** _____ 67 _____ .

The answers on this page end in "...ing."

_____ 68 _____ **ing**

_____ 69 _____ **ing**

_____ 70 _____ **ing**

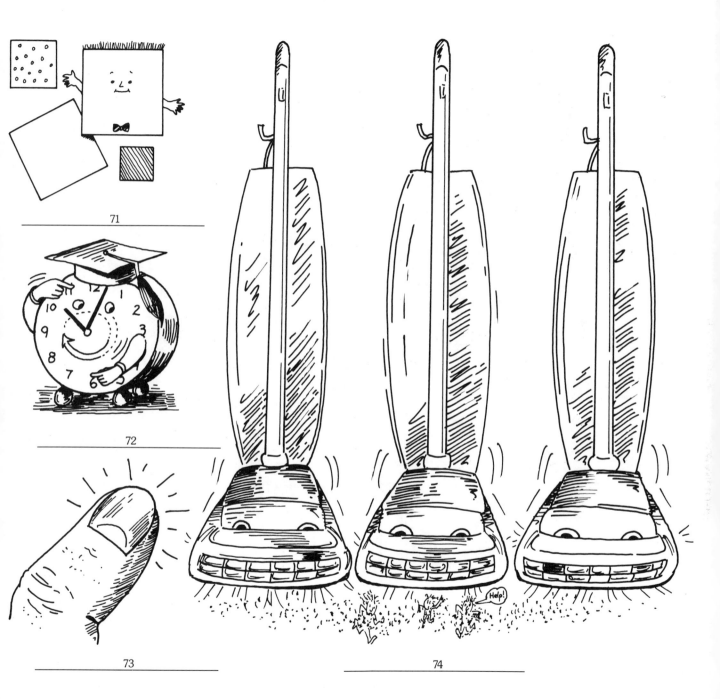

71

72

73

74

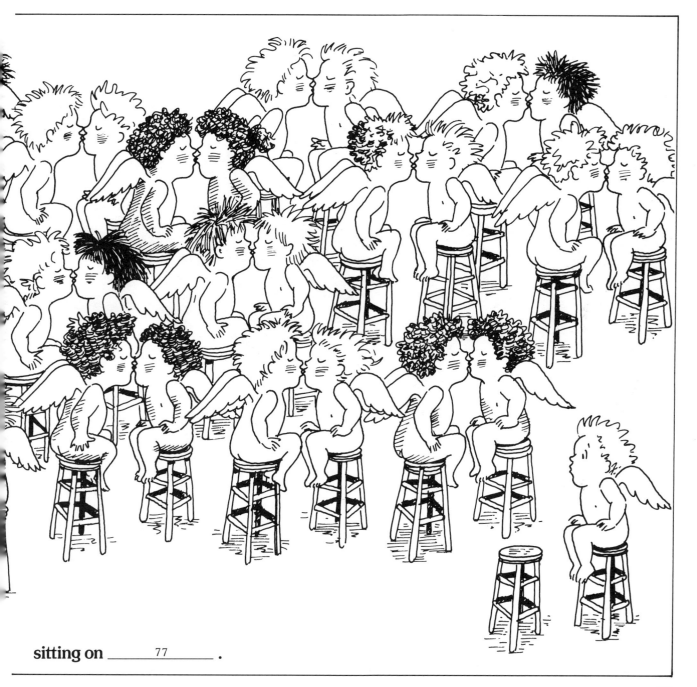

sitting on _____77_____ .

77

The Story of

Robin Hood and the Hot-Blooded Hawkers

An astounding piece of historical information was recently revealed—rock music was around as far back as in the days of Robin Hood. It turns out that Robin Hood was finding that stealing from the rich and giving to the poor was being frowned upon by the authorities.

"Don't interfere with law and order," the authorities warned.

Arrests of his social-minded companions were becoming more frequent. When questioned, R.H. offered different explanations in their defense.

"The likelihood that the rich miss what we take is awfully slim," he sometimes said.

"Surely the rich can handle a small surcharge on their possessions," he said at other times.

"I just borrowed the money," he once claimed offhandedly, referring to the sack of coins found in his possession.

Robin Hood was no longer seen as amusing. His excuses were not being tolerated and he was being publicly discredited across the countryside.

Well, it turns out that along with helping the poor, Robin Hood had a personal interest in music. Specifically, he loved rock music. Because he worried about his reputation being seriously threatened, R.H. decided to regroup his merry men into a rock band. However, he was resolved to continue helping the poor. "We'll charge the rich for our concerts," he said to his thievish companions, "and contribute what we earn to the poor."

Though this seemed like a good idea to R.H., this decision didn't sit well for all of his colleagues. Only three chose to remain, a triplet of cousins who were well intentioned enough, but who also had ghastly tempers. They argued constantly, among themselves and with others. There was Suzanne, who was so concerned with her fabulous wardrobe that she got snippy and furious whenever what she wore got the least bit dirty. (And it wasn't easy to keep perfectly clean in the forest!) There was Jeremy, who shouted loudly at any provocation, which seemed to make him prone to frequent nosebleeds. And there was Claudette, the crankiest of the three, with a generally unpleasant attitude toward everyone. Robin decided to call them the Hot-Blooded Hawkers.

Getting his rock music scheme off the ground presented some problems to Robin. Though the Hot-Blooded Hawkers were a spirited trio, they didn't have much musical background. As a matter of fact, their music was pretty terrible. Also, rock music wasn't very popular at the time. People just thought of it as a lot of noise.

But Robin Hood and his new band gave it a go. At the outset, they tried setting up their instruments in town squares and charging admission. No one came. Then they tried scheduling a large concert in a nearby pasture. They posted many advertisements to announce it. Still no one came. People not only didn't like rock music, they especially didn't like the music of Robin Hood and the Hot-Blooded Hawkers. The plan wasn't working.

R.H. was becoming discouraged, and the Hawkers' dispositions were worsening. But Robin didn't give up. He was resolved to continue aiding the poor.

Finally he thought of a solution. "We'll start a home delivery service," he said to the Hawkers, "and play concerts right outside people's houses. We'll be selective, of course, and only choose homes of the rich."

This idea seemed so ridiculous to the Hawkers that they stopped their squabbling and stared at Robin in amazement.

"That's a crazy idea for generating income," Jeremy said. "They hate our music."

"They won't come and hear our concerts now," Suzanne said. "What makes you think they'd pay to have us play right outside their windows?"

"You dumbfound me," Claudette added. "People will demand that we shut up."

"That's just the point," Robin Hood said. "We'll stop playing only after they pay us, and only when they pay us enough."

The Hawkers were skeptical, but they gave it a try. The idea worked! People gave generous sums just to have Robin Hood and the Hot-Blooded Hawkers shut up and go away. It turned out to be an excellent plan.

Robin Hood was no longer hounded by the authorities. His biggest problem was grappling with the ill-tempered cousins. Still, he felt it was worth the trouble. "With inflation being what it is," he explained when asked why he continued, "the poor can't possibly accumulate any wealth."

Getting a Computer to Help

Dedicated $1.00 word zealots have brought their computers into the act, programming them to calculate the value of whatever words they input. It takes the drudge out of testing words.

The following program is written in BASIC and will work on Apple and IBM computers with the adjustment in line 110.

```
110   TEXT: HOME (or) 110 CLS
120   PRINT
130   PRINT
140   PRINT "THE 1.00 WORD CHECKER"
150   PRINT: PRINT
160   PRINT "WHAT WORD WOULD YOU
      LIKE TO CHECK?"
170   PRINT "(TO END PROGRAM TYPE Q)"
180   INPUT A$
190   IF A$ = "Q" THEN GOTO 340
200   IF A$ = " " THEN GOTO 160
210   V = 0
220   FOR T = 1 TO LEN (A$)
230   IF MID$ (A$,T,1) < "A" OR MID$
      (A$,T,1) > "Z" THEN GOTO 160
240   V = V + ASC (MID$(A$,T,1)) − 64
250   NEXT T
260   PRINT
270   V = V/100
280   IF V = 1 THEN PRINT A$;" IS A
      $1.00 WORD!!!"
290   IF V < > 1 THEN PRINT A$;" IS A $";V;"
      WORD."
300   PRINT
310   PRINT
320   PRINT
330   GOTO 160
340   END
```